Hymns
For Home and Church

It is provided at the printing and distribution cost for members and units of the church as a convenience. It is available on Amazon in many markets around the world.
ISBN: 9798339189640

Table of Contents

** These Hymns have been moved to later pages to allow for two-page Hymns to be on the same Pages.

1001

Come, Thou Fount of Every Blessing

1 Samuel 7:7–12 | Alma 5:26–27

♩ = 63–76

1. Come, Thou Fount of ev-'ry bless-ing; Tune my heart to sing Thy grace.
2. Here I raise my Eb-e-ne-zer; Hith-er by Thy help I'm come.
3. Oh, to grace how great a debt-or Dai-ly I'm con-strained to be!

Streams of mer-cy, nev-er ceas-ing, Call for songs of loud-est praise.
And I hope, by Thy good plea-sure, Safe-ly to ar-rive at home.
Let Thy good-ness, like a fet-ter, Bind my wan-d'ring heart to Thee.

Teach me some me-lo-dious son-net, Sung by flam-ing tongues a-bove.
Je-sus sought me when a strang-er, Wan-d'ring from the fold of God;
Prone to wan-der, Lord, I feel it, Prone to leave the God I love.

Praise the mount; I'm fixed up-on it: Mount of Thy re-deem-ing love.
He, to res-cue me from dan-ger, In-ter-posed His pre-cious blood.
Here's my heart, O take and seal it; Seal it for Thy courts a-bove.

The prophet Samuel set up a great stone as a memorial to remind his people that God had saved them in battle. He called the stone "Eben-ezer," or "stone of help." (See 1 Samuel 7:10–12.)

Text: Robert Robinson, 1758; alt.
Music: American folk tune; *Wyeth's Repository of Sacred Music,*
Part Second, 1813; alt.; arr. 2024 | NETTLETON

When the Savior Comes Again

Doctrine and Covenants 45:56–59 | 1 Nephi 22:24–28

1. When the Sav-ior comes a-gain,
2. When that glo-rious day is here,

He will cleanse the earth, and then In glo-ry He will reign as King of
there will be no need to fear; For Sa-tan will be bound, and Christ will

kings a-mong all men. Hate will cease and war will end;
reign a thou-sand years. Death and pain will be no more;

peace will dwell through-out the land; The wolf shall feed to-geth-er with the
hid-den knowl-edge shall come forth And ev-'ry tongue con-fess that Christ is

1003

It Is Well with My Soul

Colossians 2:13–15 | 1 Peter 1:3–9

♩ = 48–60 Conduct in 2

1. When peace, like a riv - er, at - ten - deth my way,
2. Though Sa - tan should buf - fet, though tri - als should come,
3. My sin— oh, the bliss of this glo - ri - ous thought!—
4. O Lord, haste the day when my faith shall be sight,

When sor - rows like sea bil - lows roll— What - ev - er my
Let this blest as - sur - ance con - trol: That Christ hath re -
My sin, not in part but the whole, Is nailed to the
The heav'ns be rolled back like a scroll. The trump shall re -

lot, Thou hast taught me to say, "It is well, it is
gard - ed my help - less es - tate And hath shed His own
cross, and I bear it no more. Praise the Lord, praise the
sound, and the Lord shall de - scend; E - ven so, it is

well with my soul."
blood for my soul.
Lord, O my soul.
well with my soul.

It is well, it is well with my

soul, with my soul; It is well, it is well with my soul.

The Apostle Paul spoke of the Savior "nailing [our sins] to his cross" (see Colossians 2:13–15) and offering forgiveness to all who repent.

Text: Horatio G. Spafford, 1876
Music: Philip P. Bliss, 1876; arr. 2024 | VILLE DU HAVRE

1004

I Will Walk with Jesus

Luke 2:52 | Moses 6:34

1. Je - sus walked in wis - dom.
2. I can grow like Je - sus.
3. I will trust in Je - sus.

Je - sus grew in truth, Show - ing love to God and man ___
I will try each day— Prom - is - ing to walk His path ___
I will hear His call. He will nev - er leave me,

___ while in His youth. Je - sus wants to guide me.
___ and there to stay. Stand - ing by my Sav - ior,
e - ven when I fall. Je - sus gives me pow - er,

Je - sus shows the way, Call - ing me to come and walk with
safe with - in His care, Step by step I'll fol - low, and His
lifts and com - forts me, Help - ing me to live and grow e -

Text and music: Stephen P. Schank, 2019

1005

His Eye Is on the Sparrow

Matthew 10:29–31 | John 14:27

♩. = 46–52 Conduct in 2

Unison

1. Why should I feel dis - cour - aged? Why should the shad - ows come? Why should my heart be lone - ly And long for heav'n and home, When Je - sus is my por - tion? My con - stant Friend is He: His
2. "Let not your heart be trou - bled." His ten - der word I hear, And rest - ing on His good - ness, I lose my doubt and fear. Though by the path He lead - eth, But one step I may see: His
3. When - ev - er I am tempt - ed, When - ev - er clouds a - rise, When songs give place to sigh - ing, When hope with - in me dies, I draw the clos - er to Him; From care He sets me free: His

In the Old Testament, the word "portion" refers to an inheritance (see Psalm 119:57). "Jesus is my portion" expresses our hope in an eternal inheritance with the Lord.

Text: Civilla D. Martin, 1905
Music: Charles H. Gabriel, 1905; arr. 2024 | SPARROW
Music arr. © 2024 IRI

1006

Think a Sacred Song

Doctrine and Covenants 25:11–12 | John 14:16–18, 27

1. Think a sa-cred song; the words will give you pow'r. Think the mel-o-
2. Think a sa-cred song when scared or feel-ing bad. Hum the qui-et

dy, and in that ver-y hour Your heart and mind will o-pen to
tune when-ev-er you are sad. Your heart and mind will o-pen to

let the Spir-it in, And you will feel His com-fort a-gain.
let the Spir-it in, And you will feel His com-fort a-gain.

Text and music: Marlene Summers Merkling, 2013

As Bread Is Broken

1 Corinthians 11:23–26 | 3 Nephi 18:3–12

♩ = 52–60

1. As bread is bro-ken, we think of Thee— Thy bro-ken
2. We drink the wa-ter in mem-o-ry Of blood Thou
3. May our re-pen-tance now be sin-cere. Un-to our
4. Help us, dear Sav-ior, to take Thy name, To be like

bod-y on Cal-va-ry. May we re-mem-ber Thy suf-f'ring
spilt in Geth-sem-a-ne. Lord, wilt Thou wash us from ev-'ry
plead-ings in-cline Thine ear. We seek for-give-ness—that gift di-
Thee and Thy word pro-claim. Send us Thy Spir-it this Sab-bath

sore, With bro-ken hearts Thy grace im-plore.
stain— Our hearts and hands make clean a-gain.
vine— A change of heart, a change of mind.
day To guide us in Thy ho-ly way.

During the Last Supper, the Savior "took bread: and when he had given thanks, he brake it, and said, Take, eat: this is my body, which is broken for you: this do in remembrance of me" (1 Corinthians 11:23–24). The Savior's flesh was broken when He was brutally scourged and nailed to the cross. But in fulfillment of prophecy, none of His bones were broken (see John 19:32–36).

Text and music: Stephen A. Reynolds, 2018 | WHEELER PARK

1009

Gethsemane

Matthew 26:36–45 | Doctrine and Covenants 19:16–19

Je-sus climbed the hill   to the Gar - den still;   His

steps were heav-y and slow.   Love and a prayer took Him there to the place on-ly He could

go.   Geth - sem - a - ne!   Je - sus loves me,_____ So He

went will-ing - ly   to Geth-sem-a - ne.   He felt

all that was sad,   wick-ed, or bad, all the pain we would ev - er know.   While His

Text: Melanie M. Hoffman, 2007
Music: Melanie M. Hoffman, 2007; arr. Roger C. Hoffman, 2023
© 2007, 2023 Peace Mountain Music (ASCAP)

Bread of Life, Living Water

John 6:35, 47–51 | John 4:6–15

♩ = 72–88

1. In the Gar-den, Je-sus suf-fered Ev-'ry sin and ev-'ry woe—
2. Je-sus sac-ri-ficed His bod-y On the cross in bit-ter pain—
3. Now I come be-fore the al-tar, Of-f'ring Him my bro-ken heart,

Bleed-ing drops from ev-'ry pore, That we might for-give-ness know.
Free-ly gave His life for us So that we would live a-gain.
Seek-ing for the pre-cious gifts His A-tone-ment can im-part.

Bread of Life, Liv-ing Wa-ter, Feed my soul, fill my heart.

Lord, give me new life in Thee And make me whole— com-

plete and ho-ly— Bound to Thee e-ter-nal-ly.

Text and music: Annette W. Dickman, 2011 | HEALING GRACE

1010

Amazing Grace

2 Corinthians 12:9–10 | Moroni 10:32–33

1. A - maz - ing grace— how sweet the sound— That saved a wretch like me! I once was lost, but now am found, Was blind, but now I see.

2. The Lord has prom - ised good to me; His word my hope se - cures. He will my shield and por - tion be As long as life en - dures.

3. Through man - y dan - gers, toils, and snares I have al - read - y come. His grace has brought me safe thus far, And grace will lead me home.

This beloved hymn reminds us of Nephi's anguished cry: "O wretched man that I am!" Then, remembering the Lord's mercy, Nephi added, "My soul will rejoice in thee, my God" (2 Nephi 4:17, 30). The text of this hymn was included in an early hymnbook of The Church of Jesus Christ of Latter-day Saints, 1841.

Text: John Newton, 1779
Music: American folk tune, 19th century; arr. 2024 | NEW BRITAIN

1011

Holding Hands around the World

Alma 53:20–21 | 1 Timothy 4:12

Text and music: Janice Kapp Perry, 2001

1013

God's Gracious Love

Matthew 6:33–34 | Isaiah 12:2

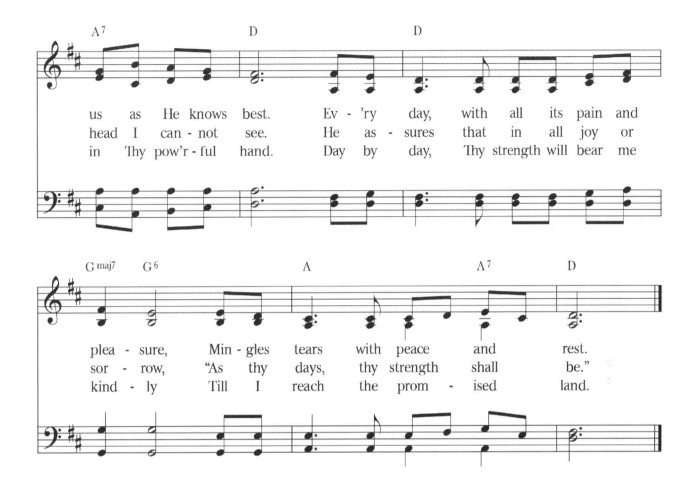

us   as   He   knows   best.   Ev - 'ry   day,   with   all   its   pain   and
head   I   can - not   see.   He   as - sures   that   in   all   joy   or
in   Thy   pow'r - ful   hand.   Day   by   day,   Thy   strength   will   bear   me

plea - sure,   Min - gles   tears   with   peace   and   rest.
sor - row,   "As   thy   days,   thy   strength   shall   be."
kind - ly   Till   I   reach   the   prom - ised   land.

Text: Lina Sandell-Berg, 1865;
English transl. Andrew L. Skoog, 1921; alt.
Music: Oscar Ahnfelt, 1872;
harm. Albert Lindström, 1885; alt. | BLOTT EN DAG

1014

My Shepherd Will Supply My Need

Psalm 23 | John 10:11–15

♩ = 92–100

C   Am   G/B   C   Am   Em

1. My Shep - herd will sup - ply my need; Je - ho - vah
2. When I walk through the shades of death, Thy pres - ence
3. The sure pro - vi - sions of my God At - tend me

F   G   C   C   G/B   Am   G/B

is His name. In pas - tures fresh He makes me
is my stay; One word of Thy sup - port - ing
all my days. O may Thy house be mine a -

C   Am   Em   F   G   C   C

feed Be - side the liv - ing stream. He brings my
breath Drives all my fears a - way. Thy hand, in
bode And all my work be praise! There would I

F   C   Dm   G   Am   F   Dm

wan - d'ring spir - it back When I for - sake His
sight of all my foes, Doth still my ta - ble
find a set - tled rest While oth - ers go and

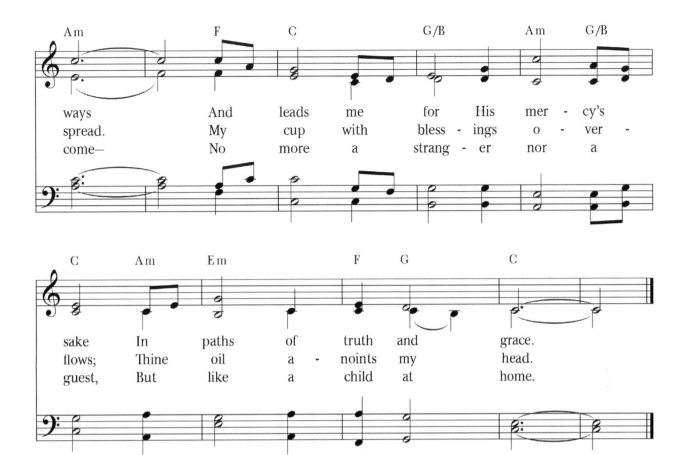

ways   And   leads   me   for   His   mer - cy's
spread.   My   cup   with   bless - ings   o - ver -
come—   No   more   a   strang - er   nor   a

sake   In   paths   of   truth   and   grace.
flows;   Thine   oil   a - noints   my   head.
guest,   But   like   a   child   at   home.

Text: Isaac Watts, 1719; based on Psalm 23
Music: American folk tune; *The Beauties of Harmony*, 1828;
arr. 2024 | RESIGNATION

1012

Anytime, Anywhere

Alma 33:4–11 | 2 Nephi 32:5

1. I can pray to my Heav'n-ly Fa - ther An - y - time, an - y - where. For
2. I can lis - ten for heav'n-ly guid-ance An - y - time, an - y - where. The

He al-ways cares, And He hears my prayers— An - y - time, an - y - where.
Spir - it will guide As I seek His light— An - y - time, an - y - where.

Text and music: Angie Killian, 2019

1015

Oh, the Deep, Deep Love of Jesus

Ephesians 3:17–19 | 1 John 4:9–10

1. Oh, the deep, deep love of Je - sus— Vast, un - mea - sured, bound - less, free—
2. Oh, the deep, deep love of Je - sus— Spread His praise from shore to shore!
3. Oh, the deep, deep love of Je - sus— Love of ev - 'ry love the best—

Roll - ing as a might - y o - cean In its full - ness o - ver me!
Praise His mer - cy, praise His good - ness; Praise His love for - ev - er - more.
'Tis an o - cean vast of bless - ing; 'Tis a ha - ven sweet of rest.

Un - der - neath me, all a - round me Is the cur - rent of His love—
How He watch - eth o'er His loved ones, Died to call them all His own;
Oh, the deep, deep love of Je - sus— 'Tis a heav'n of heav'ns to me;

Lead - ing on - ward, lead - ing home - ward To His glo - rious rest a - bove.
How for them He in - ter - ced - eth, Watch - eth o'er them from His throne.
And it lifts me up to glo - ry, Lifts me up e - ter - nal - ly.

Text: Samuel Trevor Francis, 1898; alt.
Music: Stephen M. Jones, 2023 | DEEP LOVE

1016

Behold the Wounds in Jesus' Hands

Doctrine and Covenants 6:36–37 | 3 Nephi 27:14–16

1. Be - hold the wounds in Je - sus' hands, The mark up - on His
2. Be - hold the out - stretched hands of Christ— Our Lord, who came to
3. Be - hold the wounds in Je - sus' hands. Look to your Lord and
4. Be - hold His wound - ed hands and feet! Come touch, and see, and

side, Then pon - der whom He meant to save When
save— Whose love and grace re - deem our souls And
live. He yearns to bless you with His love And
feel The wounds and marks that you may know His

on the cross He died. We can - not see the
lift us from the grave. Though we are bruised when -
all your sins for - give. Oh, emp - ty is the
love for you is real. Then as you fall to

love of God, Which saves us from the Fall, Yet
e'er we stray, His guid - ing hands ca - ress. He
heart of man When it is filled with sin. Come,
wor - ship Him And wash His feet with tears, Your

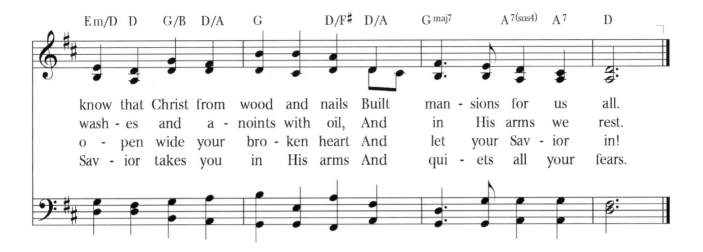

know that Christ from wood and nails Built man - sions for us all.
wash - es and a - noints with oil, And in His arms we rest.
o - pen wide your bro - ken heart And let your Sav - ior in!
Sav - ior takes you in His arms And qui - ets all your fears.

The words "Christ from wood and nails built mansions for us all" are a poetic expression that reminds us of the Savior's Crucifixion and His gift of eternal life. The Lord told His disciples: "In my Father's house are many mansions. . . . I go to prepare a place for you" (John 14:2).

Text: John V. Pearson, 1997; alt.
Music: David R. Naylor, 1998 | BEHOLD THE WOUNDS

1017

This Is the Christ

3 Nephi 11:3–17 | Luke 22:41–44

1. They heard a voice, a voice so mild. It pierced them
(2. I read His) words, the words He prayed While bear - ing

through and made their souls to quake. They saw Him come, a man in
sor - row in Geth - sem - a - ne. I feel His love, the price He

white,_____ The Sav - ior, who had suf - fered for their sake. They felt the
paid._____ How man - y drops of blood were spilled for me? With Saints of

wounds in hands and side, And each could tes - ti - fy: This is the
old in joy - ful cry I too can tes - ti - fy: This is the

Christific.
This is the Christ, the ho-ly Son of God— Our Sav-ior, Lord, Re-

deem - er of man-kind. This is the Christ, the Heal-er of our

souls, Who ran-somed us with love di - vine. 2. I read His

ran-somed us with love di - vine.

After His Resurrection, Jesus Christ visited a group of faithful people in the ancient Americas who were awaiting His prophesied appearance. Verse 1 refers to that sacred event (see 3 Nephi 11). Verse 2 describes how we feel today as we read about His great atoning sacrifice.

Text: James E. Faust and Jan Underwood Pinborough, 1995
Music: Michael Finlinson Moody, 1995; alt. | THIS IS THE CHRIST

1018

Come, Lord Jesus

Alma 7:9–13 | Luke 2:4–7

1. Come, Lord Je-sus, to the man-ger. May we see Thy ten-der
2. Come, Lord Je-sus, to the wound-ed— Bro-ken heart and bend-ed
3. Come, Lord Je-sus, great Re-deem-er, Light of Morn-ing, Prince of

face— Great Cre-a-tor, here a strang-er,
knee. Wor-thy Lamb, Thy love un-bound-ed,
Peace. We will be Thy chil-dren ev-er.

In-fant in this hum-ble place. Dark-ness scat-ter;
Bid our souls to rest in Thee. Grant us mer-cy,
Dry our tears; may weep-ing cease. Come in glo-ry;

Harmony (optional)

morn-ing swell. Come, dear Lord Im - man - u - el.
Sav - ior, King; Come with heal - ing in Thy wings.
come a - gain. Come to us to rule and reign.

Come, Lord Je - sus, to the man - ger.
Come, Lord Je - sus, to the wound - ed.
Read - y us to kneel and greet Thee.

Come, Lord Je - sus, come!
Come, Lord Je - sus, come!
Come, Lord Je - sus, come!

Text: From the Church production *Savior of the World:*
His Birth and Resurrection, 2000; alt.
Music: David A. Zabriskie, 2000 | COME, LORD JESUS
© 2000, 2024 IRI

1201

Hail the Day That Sees Him Rise

Mark 16:19 | 1 Nephi 21:14–16

♩ = 96–112

F / B♭ / C / F / B♭ / C⁷ / F

1. Hail the day that sees Him rise, Al - le - lu - ia!
2. There for Him high tri - umph waits. Al - le - lu - ia!
3. See, He lifts His hands a - bove! Al - le - lu - ia!
4. Lord, be - yond our mor - tal sight, Al - le - lu - ia!

F / B♭ / C / F / B♭ / C⁷ / F

To His throne be - yond the skies. Al - le - lu - ia!
Lift your heads, e - ter - nal gates. Al - le - lu - ia!
See, He shows the prints of love! Al - le - lu - ia!
Raise our hearts to reach Thy height. Al - le - lu - ia!

Dm / Cm / Gm / C / F / C

Christ, the Lamb for sin - ners giv'n, Al - le - lu - ia!
He has con - quered death and sin; Al - le - lu - ia!
Hark! His gra - cious gifts be - stow, Al - le - lu - ia!
There Thy face un - cloud - ed see, Al - le - lu - ia!

F / B♭ / C / F / B♭ / C⁷ / F

En - ters now the high - est heav'n. Al - le - lu - ia!
Take the King of Glo - ry in. Al - le - lu - ia!
Bless - ings on His Church be - low. Al - le - lu - ia!
Find our heav'n of heav'ns in Thee. Al - le - lu - ia!

Text: Charles Wesley, 1739; alt.
Music: Robert Williams, 1817; harm. *The English Hymnal,* 1906; alt. | LLANFAIR

Music alt. © 2024 IRI

1202

He Is Born, the Divine Christ Child

Luke 2:6–14 | Isaiah 9:6

Sing the refrain before verse 1 and after each verse.

Text: *Nouveaux Cantiques*, 1812; English transl. 2024
Music: French carol; *Airs notés du recueil de cantiques spirituels à l'usage des petits*, 1824; arr. 2024 | IL EST NÉ

1203

What Child Is This?

Luke 2:7–16 | Matthew 2:9–11

♩. = 40–46   Conduct in 2

1. What Child is this, who, laid to rest, On Mar - y's lap is
2. Why lies He in such mean es - tate, Where ox and ass are
3. So bring Him in - cense, gold, and myrrh. Come, peas - ant, king, to

sleep - ing— Whom an - gels greet with an - thems sweet, While
feed - ing? Good Chris - tians, fear, for sin - ners here The
own Him. The King of kings sal - va - tion brings; Let

shep - herds watch are keep - ing? This, this is
si - lent Word is plead - ing. Nails, spear, shall
lov - ing hearts en - throne Him. Raise, raise the

Christ, the King, Whom shep - herds guard, and an - gels sing:
pierce Him through, The cross be borne for me, for you;
song on high. The vir - gin sings her lul - la - by.

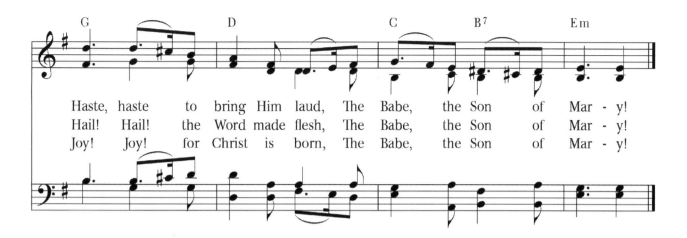

Haste, haste   to bring Him laud, The Babe,   the Son   of   Mar - y!
Hail! Hail!   the Word made flesh, The Babe,   the Son   of   Mar - y!
Joy!   Joy!   for Christ is born, The Babe,   the Son   of   Mar - y!

Text: William Chatterton Dix, 1867
Music: English melody, 16th century;
harm. John Stainer, 1867; alt. | GREENSLEEVES

1204

Star Bright

3 Nephi 1:4–21 | Helaman 14:1–7

1. The heav - ens with light o'er - flow - ing A sto - ry of love will tell. A new star will shine in glo - ry When Je - sus comes on earth to dwell.

2. Be joy - ful with eyes up - turn - ing, Be - hold - ing the time at hand. The night sign will soon be burn - ing; He's com - ing to our prom - ised land.

3. Our Fa - ther with love is send - ing The Christ child to con - quer strife. His mer - cy to all ex - tend - ing, He's bring - ing ev - er - last - ing life.

This song is written from the point of view of the people in the Book of Mormon who were looking for the prophesied signs of the Savior's birth (see Helaman 14:1–7).

Text: Lorin F. Wheelwright, 1959; alt.
Music: Lorin F. Wheelwright, 1959

Made in the USA
Las Vegas, NV
21 April 2025